The Jungle Book

A Play

Adapted by

John Hartoch

From stories by

Rudyard Kipling

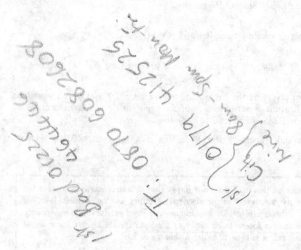

Samuel French – London
New York – Sydney – Toronto – Hollywood

THE JUNGLE BOOK

First produced by the Bristol Old Vic Theatre School, at the New Vic Studio Theatre, King Street, Bristol, on 22nd November 1983, with the following cast:

Gisborne/Head Man	Richard Coombs
Abdul Gafur/Akela	Tom Griffin
Amira/Chil the Kite	Lisa Bowerman
Elder Mowgli	Michael Corbidge
Villager/Hathi/Grey Brother	Guy Moore
Father Wolf/Priest/Buck	Ian Crowe
Mother Wolf	Anji Carroll
Tabaqui/Man/Noisy Monkey	Kean Rand
Shere Khan	Andrew Black
Baloo	Geoffrey Owen
Bagheera	Michael Brazier
Younger Mowgli	Antony Howes
Kaa	Julia Ford
Tha/2nd Monkey	Paul Rosewell
First Tiger/Head Monkey	Bryan Kennedy
Buldeo/Buck	David Hudson
Messua	Susan Tordoff

The play directed by John Hartoch

Subsequently presented by Walter Jokel for Portman Theatre Productions at the Adelphi Theatre, Strand, London on 5th December, 1984 with the following cast:

Gisborne/Hathi/Second Monkey	Jon Iles
Abdul Gafur/Bagheera	Jonathan Izard
Villager/Younger Mowgli	Emlyn Harris
Amira/Chil the Kite	Julia Lintott
Older Mowgli/Tha	David Banks
Father Wolf/Head Monkey/Priest	Gareth Tudor-Price
Mother Wolf/Indian Woman	Carol Ann Ford
Tabaqui	Jonathan Hartman
Shere Khan	Simon Cuff
Akela/First of the Tigers	Nicholas Geake
Baloo/Buldeo	Jeremy Sinden
Grey Brother/Noisy Monkey	James Mathews
Kaa	Fenella Fielding

Fourth Monkey   Conor McGivern
Messua   Catherine Shipton

The play directed by John Hartoch

Act I Scene 1 Gisborne's Verandah
        Scene 2 The Wolf Cave
        Scene 3 The Council Rock
        Scene 4 The Jungle
        Scene 5 The Bank of the River
        Scene 6 The Jungle
        Scene 7 Gisborne's Verandah

Act II Scene 1 Gisborne's Verandah
        Scene 2 The Jungle
        Scene 3 The Cold Lairs
        Scene 4 The Jungle
        Scene 5 A Jungle Path
        Scene 6 The Village
        Scene 7 The Plain
        Scene 8 The Ravine

PRODUCTION NOTES

Doubling
As may be seen from the cast-lists, doubling is essential to the nature of the piece. *It is a story being told by a group of actors who assume different roles when called upon.* As it can be done with a very large cast (the more the merrier in I, 3 and II, 3!) or with as few as thirteen it would be folly for me to offer a definitive doubling list. To attempt it with fewer than thirteen is not recommended as the more crowded scenes become too thin and I, 5 becomes very nearly impossible!

Set   Shadows - Play?
In order that the actors should be as comfortable and confident as possible some form of stage-padding is essential. In Bristol we used rubberized horse-hair, in London pile carpeting. The rest of the set should consist of an upper level for Gisborne's balcony and various important focusings (Kaa, Mowgli in II, 8, etc.), and a number of other levels which could be supplied simply by rostra, or, as we did at Bristol, with scaffolding and "shelves" (see illustration). The important thing is to make the Jungle functional, not naturalistic, so that we are always aware of the actors telling the story. A central platform for Akela's rock is essential. Gisborne's verandah should be made as real as possible within the overall style.   Army camoflage

Costume
For the Gisborne scenes costume and props should be completely realistic. For the Jungle scenes the animal costumes should be easy to move in and should not suggest too strongly any particular animal (with exceptions as given in the Costume List, page vii). Let the actors create the animal characters through their bodies, their faces and voices. Don't be tempted to do it for them. For the scenes in the Indian village "quick-change" dhotis, saris and turbans are easily made.

Props
For the Gisborne scenes, realistic. For most of the Jungle scenes, mimed. For certain moments in the Jungle (I, 5) and for the village use very obvious props. All such items as jewellery for villagers, fire-pot, shovel, hoe, food-basket, etc. we formalized by painting them black. The reason for these levels is to accentuate the difference between "present time" (Gisborne scenes) and "flashback" and, once again, to underline the story-telling element. It may be felt advisable to mime all props apart from those in the Gisborne scenes, but, having tried this, I decided there was something to be gained by having the human beings surrounded by objects and possessions, thereby contrasting them with animals. Equally I wanted to be able to mime

a bed, or a fire-brand without the audience feeling it to be awkward, so the formalized props helped, enabling Mowgli, for instance, to take a totally imaginary fire-brand from a very solid fire-pot without it seeming wrong.

Special Effects

The "faces in the dark" for I,1; II,5 and II,8 are achieved by the actors each having a small torch which they train on their faces.

For a small, or medium-sized theatre, it is exciting and satisfying to have all the sounds acoustically or vocally made. Perhaps not everyone will be able to find or afford live sitar and tabla-players and may have to fall back on recorded music but all the animal noises can be made by human agency. A few hours experimenting with the cast will produce impressive cicadas, tree-frogs, wolves and other unidentifiable but undeniably "jungly" noises. A good "baby" is essential to help create the illusion of the baby Mowgli in I,2 and I,3. The "tiger" is more difficult, the best sound being achieved by an inhalation through a sort of croak at the back of the throat, but practice is necessary if the actor is not to lose his voice. The fire can be suggested by the simple method of slapping two fingers against an extended palm; the echo effect by having other actors repeat exactly the last syllables and intonation of each phrase of Mowgli and Shere Khan (II, 8).

The "chant" in I,5 should be something which conjures up primeval movements, not specifically Indian in its feel. We used a simple Indian folk-song tune, gave it a strong bass-feeling and sang it in 5ths, so that we ended up with something sounding like a synthesis between Hindu, Red Indian and Gregorian chant!! The Road Song of the Bandar-Log (II,3) should sound like so many wooden spoons beating on tin kettles. The snake's dance should be weird and willowy.

The misnamed "sitar chord" at the end of scenes refers to the run of the scale played by a sitarist at the start of a raga.

Movement and Mime

A great deal of time and effort must be spent on movement. Observing and imitating the animals is essential to the success of the piece. In my productions I had the invaluable assistance of a mime-artist (Geoffrey Buckley) but also a great deal was achieved by the actors themselves. The necessity for the monkey-fight in the second act to be exciting and athletic cannot be stressed enough.

The death of Shere Khan was achieved by the actor concerned falling off a level into the arms of a group of catchers who entered at the last moment for this purpose. In London Simon Cuff threw himself (none too cheerfully at first!) off a nine-foot level and was never dropped, but this is not to be attempted without expert training. In Bristol Andrew Black fell off a level only four-foot high, and in a small theatre this was quite acceptable.

Short Version

The first version of this play, with which we toured schools in Avon and Stroud, lasted 75 minutes, had a set consisting of a children's climbing-frame and a large piece of matting, and was considered suitable for seven-to-eleven-year-olds. To discover this script within the full-length one, simply get rid of the Gisborne scenes (I,1; I,7; II,1; II,2), start at "Now Chil the Kite ..." (page 4), cut from line on page 10 (Scene 4) to line page 17 (Scene 5) and have cast and Shere Khan recite final poem without the activity from Mowgli, Abdul and Amira (II,8).

J.G.H.

COSTUMES

ACT I

SCENE 1
Gisborne: jodhpurs, jacket, shirt, cravat, boots
Abdul: white turban, breeches, jacket, contrasting sash, dagger, bare feet
Older Mowgli: loin-cloth with hunting-knife
Villager: white turban, shirt, dhoti

SCENE 2
Cast in standard animal costumes, ranging from grey to sandy brown
Specials—**Tabaqui:** sandy yellow
  Shere Khan: dull orange with faded stripes on back

SCENE 3
Baloo: brown with some padding
Bagheera: black with a blue sheen

SCENE 4
Mowgli: actor removes top of his basic animal costume and plays with torso
  naked. Since Mowgli is meant to be naked until Scene 6 of Act II this
  seems the best way of expressing it while distinguishing him sufficiently
  from the beasts

SCENE 5
First of the Tigers: sandy-coloured costume with black stripes, the latter
  velcro'ed so that sandy-coloured strips can be overlaid. When Tiger gets
  stripes, the Chorus, as creepers, remove strips revealing black stripes
Men: white dhotis and turbans

SCENE 6
Kaa: hood, long dress decorated with python-markings, skirt slit up sides to
  hip-level. Lycra tights in complementary colour. Bare feet

SCENE 7
Amira: orange sari

ACT II

<small>Scenes 5 and 6</small>

Villagers: longish, loose shirts for the men, with turbans and dhotis. All dhotis white, some shirts coloured. Saris and cholis for women in yellow, russet, orange, tan. Copper and brass bangles

Buldeo: long, loose shirt in striped material. No turban. Tiger-tooth necklace. Sash

Priest: white, long dhoti. Bare head and torso. Silk braid (white) over shoulder

Messua: white sari and choli. Gold sandals. No jewellery

ACT I

SCENE 1

The verandah of Gisborne's bungalow in a clearing in the Indian jungle. Evening

The bungalow is set C on an upper level, as naturalistic as possible. Far left is a statue of Krishna, far right a statue of a demon with an elephant's head. The interior of the bungalow is suggested by a curtain through which people entering from the house must pass. There are the remains of a meal on a small table. Gisborne sits at the cluttered table, occasionally sipping from a glass at his elbow. A young girl's voice is heard, off, singing a plaintive Indian song which Gisborne is enjoying. The song breaks off with a slap and a cry

Gisborne Abdul! Abdul!

Abdul enters; a middle-aged, Muslim butler

Abdul Sahib?
Gisborne Your daughter has a beautiful voice, Abdul. Why won't you let her sing?
Abdul Ha! She is a dreamer, Sahib. She sings and forgets her work. I make her remember her work.
Gisborne Must you beat her so frequently?
Abdul Am I not her father, Sahib?
Gisborne (*one last try*) It would please me to hear her cries less often.
Abdul (*pouring Gisborne another drink; with a gesture of barely-disguised contempt*) Yes, Sahib. When I beat her you shall not hear. Thank you, Sahib. (*He makes to go*)

A Hindu villager appears, breathless from running

Villager Gisborne, Sahib! The Red One!! The Red One has killed a man!!
Gisborne Abdul! Who?
Villager A forest guard. I do not know his name. By the Kanye stream. His head smashed—poh!—like an egg!

Abdul hands Gisborne his rifle. Gisborne checks it

Gisborne The Red One. I knew he'd turn to man in time. There's plenty of game about, even for him. This must have been done for devilry.
Abdul Yes, Sahib. He is the very devil!
Gisborne Let's see now. He lies up in the rocks at the back of the sal trees.

Villager Not now, Sahib. Now he will be raging to and fro.
Abdul Yes, Sahib. Remember the first kill is a triple kill always. Man-blood makes them mad. He may be in the thicket now, even as we speak.

They look towards the thicket. A growling noise. Gisborne raises his gun

Older Mowgli emerges from the thicket, growling. He laughs

Older Mowgli Fear not. The tiger that killed has gone to drink, and now he is asleep under a rock behind the hill. He will not wake again.
Gisborne You killed him? Where is the skin?
Older Mowgli Not worth the taking.
Gisborne The whiskers? Do you not take the whiskers?
Older Mowgli I? Am I a lousy shikaree of the Jungle to set flame to a tiger's whiskers? Let him lie. Chil, the Kite, shall eat his fill today.
Gisborne Where is your gun?
Older Mowgli Ah! My gun! May I see the Sahib's?
Abdul Do not trust him with it, Sahib. He is a thieving jungle gypsy.

Gisborne offers the gun. Mowgli takes it, with a hard look at Abdul

Older Mowgli Arré! It is very fine. But I need no such weapon. I have just as good. (*He draws his hunting knife*)
Gisborne You killed a tiger with that?
Older Mowgli He was sleeping. I jumped on his back, pulled back his head. For a moment he knew, then . . . (*he gestures*) . . . a dog's death for a dog.

Gisborne nods to the Villager to ascertain the truth

The Villager vanishes

Older Mowgli He will find it as I say.
Gisborne If he does, and you killed a tiger with nothing but a hunting knife, you are a man who could be useful to me. I am the warden of the forests of this area. Would you work for me? For the Government? For Queen Victoria?
Older Mowgli (*laughing*) I have heard of this great Queen Vittoria. But in the Jungle I am King. Should a king work for a queen?
Gisborne But there are other things . . . money . . . a pension . . .
Older Mowgli Money is stupid. It breeds hatred and killing between men. May I come in, Sahib? I have never yet looked within a white man's house.

Gisborne motions him to enter. He does so on tiptoe. Abdul keeps a close watch. Mowgli looks into the next room

Ha! That is a bed. For sleeping. I have seen such a thing before. (*Looking at the bottle*) And this . . . this is the drink that makes fools out of men.
Gisborne Not exactly. The men are fools already. The drink just shows them for what they are.
Older Mowgli Can the Sahib not be what he is without the help of this?

The Villager dashes in. He stares at Mowgli

Gisborne Well?

Villager It is true, Sahib. The Red One is dead. His throat is cut. It is magic, Sahib! A great magic!!

Mowgli looks at him

The Villager raises his hands to ward off the magic and runs off

Older Mowgli It is as I said. There are many rich things here. Is the Sahib not afraid that he may be robbed? I have never seen such a gun.

Abdul Only a thief from the Jungle would rob here.

Mowgli stares at him, then smiles

Older Mowgli In the village where once I lived it was the custom when a goat bleated too loud to cut its throat. But have no fear. I am going.

Gisborne Wait. One moment. I do not know your name.

Older Mowgli I am called Mowgli.

Gisborne Mowgli . . .?

Older Mowgli The Frog. So I was named by my mother, Raksha.

Abdul Raksha! The Demon!! Sahib this is indeed not a gypsy but a devil!

Gisborne Leave us will you, Abdul.

Abdul But Sahib . . .

Gisborne Leave us. I shall be all right. I have my gun and you are within call.

Abdul Sahib.

Abdul goes, with a warning glance at Mowgli

Gisborne Will you talk, Mowgli?

Older Mowgli A man must talk sometimes with other men. There are none in the Jungle. (*He sits*) Tell me, Sahib, why does a man like you, a man with servants, a man with money, a man with a gun—why does such a man need this drink which takes away his manhood?

Gisborne Oh, it's not as bad as all that, Mowgli. It only makes men foolish when they drink too much.

Older Mowgli And the Sahib does not drink too much?

Gisborne I'm a long way from home, Mowgli, a long way from my own people.

Older Mowgli Ah! This I understand. Once I, too, longed for my home. When first I lived amongst men.

Gisborne You mean you had a home which was not amongst men?

Older Mowgli Indeed, Sahib. My home was in the Jungle, as it is now. And my friends. . . . The tale is a long one but this night is a night for talking and if the Sahib wishes he shall hear.

Gisborne Please.

Older Mowgli Ha! Where to begin?

The Lights begin to fade as the sun sets

I am no teller of tales. The start I do not remember. My mother, Raksha, told me of it in later years. It seems it was at this season, a night such as this between the time when the sun dies and the moon rises. And on that night also a tiger hunted Man before his Night was upon him.

Gisborne His Night?

Older Mowgli Have patience, Sahib. See! The sun goes down. Let us watch it sink. Then I shall tell thee.

Black-out. A low drumbeat

A Face appears high in the darkness (see Production Notes), descending as it speaks. After the first two lines other Faces appear, rising from below. On the fifth line a spoken "round" begins, the cast being divided into groups, Faces appearing and disappearing and each group resting the verse while a howl is heard. As each group finishes the Faces vanish. The first Face repeats the final sentence

Face 1	Now Chil the Kite brings home the night
	That Mang the Bat sets free—
Face 2	The herds are shut in byre and hut
Face 3	For loosed till dawn are we.
Groups	This is the hour of pride and power
	Talon and tush and claw.
	Oh hear the call! (*Howl*) Good hunting all
	That keep the Jungle Law!

As Face 1 repeats the final sentence, the Lights come up on 1st Narrator

Face 1 sees him and scuttles away

SCENE 2

The Wolf Cave

Actors must establish the cave area, the cave entrance, the ledge outside the cave

The Lights come up on the lower (non-naturalistic) "Jungle" level revealing Mother and Father Wolf. All other cast, except Shere Khan and Tabaqui are up stage on different levels with their backs to us. Cast make jungle sounds. 1st Narrator looks around at the Jungle then begins

1st Narrator It was seven o'clock of a very warm evening in the Seonee Hills when Father Wolf woke up from his day's rest, yawned, and spread his paws out one after the other to get rid of the sleepy feeling in their tips.

2nd Narrator turns and speaks

2nd Narrator Mother Wolf lay with her big, grey nose dropped across her four, tumbling, squealing cubs, and the moon shone into the mouth of the cave where they all lived.

Father Wolf Aurgh! It is time to hunt again.

Tabaqui enters, sniffs, comes to the cave mouth

Tabaqui Good luck go with you, O Chief of the Wolves; and good luck and strong, white teeth go with the noble children, that they may never forget the hungry in the world.

During the following the cast turn round, as they speak their lines, to watch the scene. The narration should flow but each Narrator should register as an individual. Diagonal lines mark division of narration as used in production. From this point narration is given to suitable cast-members, and the designation "Narrator" refers to whomsoever is chosen to do that particular piece

Narrator It was the jackal/Tabaqui/the dish-licker/and the wolves of India despise Tabaqui/because he runs about making mischief/and telling tales/ and eating rags/and pieces of leather from the village rubbish-heaps./But they are afraid of him too/because Tabaqui/more than anyone else in the Jungle/is apt to go mad/and then he forgets that he was ever afraid of anyone/and runs through the forest biting everything in his way./Even the tiger runs and hides when little Tabaqui goes mad./

Father Wolf Enter then, and look. But there is no food here.

Tabaqui For a wolf, no, but for so mean a person as myself a dry bone is a good feast. Who are we, the Jackal People, to pick and choose?

Narrator He scuttled to the back of the cave where he found the bone of a buck with some meat on it.

Tabaqui All thanks for this good meal.

Cub-noises from the Chorus members

How beautiful are the noble children. How large are their eyes. And so young too. Indeed, indeed I might have remembered that the children of kings are men from the beginning.

Narrator Tabaqui knew as well as anyone else that there is nothing so unlucky as to compliment children to their faces;/and it pleased him to see Mother and Father Wolf look uncomfortable.

Tabaqui Shere Khan, the tiger, has shifted his hunting-grounds. He will hunt among these hills for the next moon. So he has told me.

Father Wolf He has no right! By the Law of the Jungle he has no right to change his quarters without due warning. He will frighten every head of game within ten miles, and I, I have to kill for two these days.

Mother Wolf His mother did not call him "Lungri—the Lame One" for nothing. He has been lame in one foot since his birth. That is why he has only killed cattle. Now the villagers of the Waingunga are angry with him, and he has come to make our villagers angry. They will scour the Jungle for him when he is far away and we and our children must run when the grass is set alight. Indeed we are very grateful to Shere Khan.

Tabaqui Shall I tell him of your gratitude?

Father Wolf (*chasing him out*) Out!! Out and hunt with thy master. Thou has done enough harm for one night!

Tiger noises from Shere Khan (off) and cast (on)

Tabaqui I go. Ye can hear Shere Khan below in the thickets. I might have saved myself the message.

Tabaqui exits

Father Wolf The fool! To begin a night's work with that noise. Does he think that our bucks are like his fat Waingunga bullocks?

Mother Wolf Hssh! It is neither buck nor bullock he hunts tonight. It is Man.

The tiger noises grow

Father Wolf Man! Faugh! Are there not enough beetles and frogs in the tanks that he must eat Man?

Tiger noises grow to a roar and break off in a howl of pain

Mother Wolf He has missed. What is it?

Father Wolf The fool has had no more sense than to jump at a woodcutter's camp-fire, and he has burned his feet. Tabaqui is with him.

Mother Wolf Something is coming up the hill. Get ready.

Father Wolf Man? A man's cub. Look!

Father Wolf and Narrator establish the position of the (invisible) baby. Baby noises from one of the chorus

Narrator Directly in front of him, holding on by a low branch, stood a naked, brown baby who could just walk—he looked up into Father Wolf's face and laughed.

Mother Wolf Is that a man's cub? Bring it here.

Father Wolf gingerly picks up the "baby". The baby noises become distressed. He takes the "baby" into the cave and puts it down. Cub noises

How little! How naked!

Angry baby noise

How bold! Ahai!

Noises of baby disturbing cubs

He is taking his place with the others. So this is a man's cub. Now was there ever a wolf could boast of a man's cub among her children?

Father Wolf I have heard now and then of such a thing, but never in our pack or in my time. He is altogether without hair and I could kill him with a touch of my foot. But see, he looks up and is unafraid.

Tabaqui (*off*) My Lord, my Lord, it went in here.

Shere Khan and Tabaqui enter

Father Wolf runs from the cave and meets the tiger

Father Wolf Shere Khan does us great honour. What does Shere Khan need?

Shere Khan My quarry. A man's cub went this way. Its parents have run off. Give it to me.

Father Wolf The Wolves are a free people. They take orders from the Head of the Pack and not from any striped cattle-killer. The man's cub is ours— to kill if we choose.

Shere Khan Ye choose and ye do not choose! What talk is this of choosing? By the bull that I killed, am I to stand nosing into your dog's den for my fair dues? It is I, Shere Khan, who speak!!

Mother Wolf (*attacking Shere Khan's rear from the cave mouth*) And it is I, Raksha—the Demon—who answer! The man's cub is mine, Lungri—mine, to me! He shall not be killed. He shall live to hunt with the pack; and in the end, look you, hunter of little naked cubs—frog-eater—fish-killer—he shall hunt thee! Now get hence or back thou goest to thy mother lamer than ever thou camest into the world! Go!!

Shere Khan Each dog barks in his own yard! We will see what the Pack will say to this fostering of man-cubs. The cub is mine, and to my teeth he will come in the end, O bush-tailed thieves.

Shere Khan and Tabaqui exit

Mother Wolf collapses, panting

Father Wolf Shere Khan speaks this much truth. The cub must be shown to the pack. Wilt thou still keep him, Mother?

Mother Wolf moves back into the cave. Cub and baby sounds

Mother Wolf Keep him! He came naked, by night and alone; yet he was not afraid. Look, he has pushed one of my babes to one side already. And that lame butcher would have killed him and would have run off to the Waingunga while the villagers here hunted through all our lairs in revenge! Keep him? Assuredly I will keep him. Lie still, little frog. Oh thou Mowgli, for Mowgli—the frog—I will call thee—the time will come when thou wilt hunt Shere Khan as he has hunted thee.

Father Wolf But what will the Pack say?

Tableau. A "broken chord" on the sitar. The Lights snap bright. Energetic movement as actors take their places

SCENE ~~3~~ 2

The Council Rock

The set and actors must establish Akela's Rock, the circle of Wolves, an area in the centre for cubs

Narrator The Law of the Jungle lays down clearly that as soon as a wolf's cubs are old enough to stand on their feet he must bring them to the Pack Council in order that the other wolves may identify them./Father Wolf waited until his cubs could run a little, and then on the night of the Pack Meeting took them and Mowgli and Mother Wolf to the Council Rock/

The Lights fade to moonlight

A hilltop covered with stones and boulders where a hundred wolves could hide./

Akela Akela, the great, grey, Lone Wolf who led the pack by strength and
cunning, lay out at full length on his rock.

Narrator And below him sat forty or more wolves of every size and colour./

Cub noises

There was very little talking at the Rock. The cubs tumbled over each
other in the centre of the circle where their mothers and fathers sat,/and
now and again a senior wolf would go quietly up to a cub, look at him
carefully, and return to his place on noiseless feet./Sometimes a mother
would push her cub far out into the moonlight, to be sure that he had not
been overlooked./Akela from his rock would cry./

Akela Ye know the Law—ye know the Law. Look well, O Wolves!

Mothers Look well! Look well, O Wolves!

Narrator And the anxious mothers would take up the cry./At last—and
Mother Wolf's neck-bristles lifted as the time came—Father Wolf pushed
"Mowgli the Frog" into the centre——

Baby noises

—where he sat laughing and playing with some pebbles in the moonlight.

Akela Look well, O Wolves.

Shere Khan (*off; from the back of the auditorium*) The cub is mine! Give him
to me. What have the free people to do with a man's cub?

Akela Look well, O Wolves! What have the Free People to do with the
orders of any save the Free People? Look well!

Unease among the Wolves

Young Wolf What have the Free People to do with a man's cub?

Old Wolf What does the Law say?

Wolves The Law! What does the Law say?

Akela What does the Law say, Baloo?

Narrator The only other creature who is allowed at the Pack Council——

Baloo Baloo, the sleepy brown bear who teaches the wolf-cubs the Law of
the Jungle——

Narrator —rose up on his hindquarters and grunted.

Baloo The Law of the Jungle says that if there is any dispute in such a
matter the cub must be spoken for by at least two members of the Pack
who are not his father and mother.

Akela Who speaks for this cub?

Shere Khan roars, off

Among the Free People, who speaks?

Silence

Baloo None? Then I will speak for the man's cub. There is no harm in a
man's cub. I have no gift of words but I speak the truth. Let him run with
the Pack, and be entered with the others. I myself will teach him.

Akela We need yet another. Baloo has spoken. Who speaks besides Baloo?

Bagheera drops into the circle. The Wolves react

Narrator A black shadow dropped down into the circle.

Bagheera It was Bagheera, the black panther.

Narrator As cunning as Tabaqui,/as bold as the wild buffalo, as reckless as the wounded elephant,/but with a voice as smooth as wild honey and a skin softer than down.

Bagheera Oh Akela, and ye the Free People, I have no right in your assembly; but the Law of the Jungle says that if there is a doubt which is not a killing matter in regard to a new cub, the life of that cub may be bought at a price. And the Law does not say who may or may not pay that price. Am I right?

Wolves (*severally*) Good! Good! Listen to Bagheera. The cub can be bought for a price. It is the Law.

Bagheera To kill a naked cub is shame. Besides, he may make better sport for you when he is grown. Baloo has spoken on his behalf. Now to Baloo's word I will add one bull, and a fat one, newly killed, not half a mile from here if ye will accept the man's cub according to the Law. Is it difficult?

Wolves What matter? He will die in the winter rains. He will scorch in the sun. What harm can a naked frog do us? Let him run with the pack. Where is the bull, Bagheera?

Bagheera Down the hill where the stream bends.

All exit, except Mother Wolf, Father Wolf, Akela, Baloo and Bagheera

Akela (*with irony*) Look well, O Wolves!

Shere Khan (*off*) The cub is mine! To my teeth will he come!!

Bagheera Ay, roar well! For the time comes when this naked thing will make thee roar to another tune, or I know nothing of Man.

Akela (*to Baloo*) Take him away. And train him as befits one of the Free People.

Tableau—sitar chord

SCENE 4 3

Mother Wolf, Father Wolf and Akela exit

Bagheera sleeps. Daylight Baloo begins to recite the Jungle Law

Baloo Now this is the Law of the Jungle—as old and as true as the sky.
And the wolf that shall keep it may prosper, but the wolf that shall break it must die.
As the creeper that girdles the tree-trunk the Law runneth forward and back—
For the strength of the Pack is the Wolf, and the strength of the Wolf is the Pack.

Cubs enter, gradually joining in

Baloo⎫
Cubs⎬ Wash daily from nose-tip to tail-tip; drink deeply but never too deep;

And remember the night is for hunting, and forget not
the day is for sleep.
The Jackal may follow the Tiger, but cub, when thy
whiskers are grown,
Remember the Wolf is a hunter—go forth and get food
of thine own.

Younger Mowgli joins the cubs

Cubs ⎫ Keep peace with the Lords of the Jungle—the Tiger, the
Younger Mowgli ⎰ Panther, the bear;
And trouble not Hathi the silent, and mock not the boar
in his lair.
When ye fight with a Wolf of the Pack, ye must fight him
alone and afar,
Lest others take part in the quarrel and the Pack be
diminished by war.

One by one the wolf cubs drift away. Only Mowgli's bored voice is heard

Younger Mowgli The lair of the Wolf is his refuge, and where he has made
him his home,
Not even the Head Wolf may enter, not even the council
may come.

....

By now Baloo is asleep

Younger Mowgli If ye kill before midnight be silent, and wake not the
woods with your bay . . .
Baloo? Baloo!!
Baloo (*waking*) Hmmm? "If ye kill before midnight be silent . . ."
Younger Mowgli Baloo! Enough! For one moment enough!
Baloo What is it, Little Brother?
Younger Mowgli Baloo, why must I learn the Law? It is dry like the earth
and I thirst for water not dust.
Baloo Ah, Mowgli, thou shouldst know that the Law is like the Giant
Creeper. It drops across everyone's back and no-one can escape it.
Younger Mowgli Shere Khan ignores it when it suits him.
Baloo Nevertheless, soon it may be that thou wilt see how all the Jungle
obeys at least one Law, and it will be no pleasant sight.
Younger Mowgli How shall that be?
Baloo Little Brother, I am hungry and thirsty. Fetch me a wild yam.
Younger Mowgli (*laughing*) Nay, Old Blind One, dost thou not know that
the wild yams are tough and dry this season?
Baloo Then let us go swim in the deep pool below the bee-rocks.
Younger Mowgli Nay, I swim there no longer. The foolish water is all going
away and I do not wish to break my head when I dive.
Baloo That is thy loss. A small crack might let in some wisdom. Still
perhaps it will not happen. We must wait and see how the mohwa blooms.

Now, where were we? Ah, yes ... "If ye kill before midnight be silent ..."

Younger Mowgli If ye kill before midnight be silent, and wake not the
woods with your bay
Lest ye frighten the deer from the crops and the Brothers
go empty away.
Ye may kill for yourself and your mates, and your cubs
as they need and ye can,
But kill not for pleasure of killing, and seven times
NEVER KILL MAN.

*Younger Mowgli continues to recite sotto voce while the Narrators take over.
During the following passages the cast perform choreographed removal of any
"Jungle" scenery (hanging creepers) to leave a bare set. Also two sides of a
river must be established*

Narrator That spring the mohwa tree that Baloo was so fond of, never
flowered. The greeny, cream-coloured, waxy blossoms were heat-killed
before they were born, and when he stood on his hind legs and shook the
tree, only a few, bad-smelling petals came down./Then, inch by inch, the
untempered heat crept into the heart of the Jungle ...

The Lights become brighter

... turning it yellow, brown, and at last black./The birds and the monkey-
people went North early in the year, for they knew what was coming,/and
the deer and the wild pig broke far away to the perished fields of the
villages, dying sometimes before the eyes of men too weak to kill them./
Mowgli, who had never known what real hunger meant, hunted for deep-
boring grubs under the bark of trees,/robbed the wasps of their new
broods/and scraped out of deserted rock-hives honey, three years old,
black as a sloe and dusty with sugar./And the heat went on and on, and
sucked up all the moisture, till at last the main channel of the Waingunga
was the only stream that carried a trickle of water between its dead banks.

Hathi enters on the higher level

Hathi And when Hathi, the Elephant, who lives for a hundred years and
more, saw a long, lean blue ridge of rock show dry in the very centre of the
stream, he knew that he was looking at the Peace Rock.

Narrator And then and there he lifted up his trunk and proclaimed the
Water Truce, as his father, before him, had proclaimed it fifty years
before.

Hathi   The stream is shrunk—the pool is dry,
And we be comrades, thou and I ...

Voices take up the cry

SCENE 5

The Bank of the River

Animals enter—Hathi, Baloo, Deer, Fawn, Wolves—upstage

All   The stream is shrunk—the pool is dry
And we be comrades, thou and I;
With fevered jowl and dusty flank
Each jostling each along the bank;
And by one droughty fear made still
Foregoing thought of quest or kill.
Now 'neath his dam the fawn may see
The lean pack-wolf as cowed as he,
And the tall buck, unflinching, note
The fangs that tore his father's throat.
The pools are shrunk—the streams are dry,
And we be playmates, thou and I,
Till yonder cloud—good hunting!—loose
The rain that breaks our Water Truce.

Younger Mowgli and Bagheera enter last of all

Bagheera wanders into the stream. Some consternation from the others

Bagheera We are under one Law indeed. Good hunting, all you of my blood! But for the Law it would be good hunting indeed.

Deer The Truce! Remember the Truce!!

Hathi Peace there, peace! The Truce holds, Bagheera. This is no time to talk of hunting.

Bagheera Who should know better than I? I have become an eater of turtles—a fisher of frogs. Ngyaah! Would I could get good from chewing branches.

Fawn We wish so very greatly.

Bagheera Well spoken, little Bud-horn. When the truce ends that will be remembered in thy favour.

Deer If any of us live through the Truce. We die like butterflies in the cold season.

Mother Wolf The Men-folk too. They die beside their ploughs and their oxen with them.

Baloo The river has fallen since last night. O Hathi, hast thou ever seen the like.

Hathi It will pass. It will pass.

Baloo We have one here that cannot endure long.

Younger Mowgli I? I have no long fur to cover my bones. But if thy hide were taken off, Baloo . . .

Baloo Never have I been seen without my hide! It is not seemly to talk in such a fashion. It is not good to make a jest of thy teacher.

Shere Khan and Tabaqui enter, moving to the downstage bank

Shere Khan Not good! What would ye have?

Tabaqui That naked thing running to and fro pulls the best of us by the whiskers for sport.

Shere Khan The Jungle has become a whelping-ground for naked cubs now. Look at me, Man-cub.

Mowgli stares. Shere Khan turns away

Man-cub this and Man-cub that! He is neither man nor cub or he would fear me tonight. Next season I shall have to beg his leave for a drink. (*He drinks*)

Bagheera That may come ... Faugh! Shere Khan! What blood is this that you bring to defile the water?

Shere Khan Man. I killed an hour since.

Reactions. The animals look to Hathi

Hathi The kill was for sport—or for food?

Shere Khan For sport. It was my Right and my Night. Thou knowest, O Hathi. Now I come to drink and make me clean again.

Hathi Hast thou drunk thy fill?

Shere Khan For tonight, yes.

Hathi Go then. None but the lame tiger would so have boasted of his Right at this season when Man and Jungle peoples suffer together. Clean or unclean, get to thy lair, Shere Khan!

Shere Khan leaves

Younger Mowgli What is this right Shere Khan speaks of? To kill Man is always shameful.

Bagheera Ask Hathi. I do not know, Little Brother.

Younger Mowgli What is Shere Khan's right, O Hathi?

Hathi It is an old tale, a tale older than the Jungle. Keep silence along the bank and I will tell it.

The animals fall silent. The Lights fade to a spot on Hathi and Mowgli on the upper level

Ye know, children, that of all things ye most fear Man. And yet ye do not know why. This is the reason. In the beginning of the Jungle, and none know when that was, the Lord of the Jungle was Tha, the First of the Elephants ...

Atmospheric lighting. The Chorus chant. The Actor positioned by the Demon statue R removes the elephant mask from it. In time with the chant he puts it on his head, then removes the "stone" latex covering to reveal a jewel-studded, sumptuous mask

He drew the Jungle out of the deep waters with his trunk; and where he made furrows in the ground with his tusk, there the rivers ran.

The Chorus unroll the fabric "rivers"

And where he stuck his foot there rose ponds of good water.

The Chorus spread the fabric "pool"

And when he blew through his trunk, the trees fell.

The Chorus take-up the stylized branches. Tha blows. The Chorus collapse the stylized branches

In those days, we of the Jungle walked together.

*The Chorus form with branches and idealized hand-held animal masks. They
dance to the chant, in a tight group*

Having no fear of each other. There was no drought, and leaves and
flowers and fruit grew together on the same trees and we ate nothing but
them. And the Jungle People knew nothing of Man, but lived together in
peace. Yet presently they began to dispute over their food, though there
was plenty for all.

Dance—the Chorus "dispute"

Tha, the first of the elephants, was busy making new jungles and leading
the rivers in their beds. He could not walk in all places; therefore he made
as the master and judge of the Jungle—the First of the Tigers.

Tha exits

*Chant. The Actor positioned by the Krishna statue turns, takes the tiger mask
from beneath statue's foot, puts it on, removes cover revealing idealized tiger
mask*

In those days the First of the Tigers was in colour all over like the blossom
of the yellow creeper, with never a stripe nor bar upon his hide. All the
Jungle People came before him without fear.

Tiger sits in judgment. Dance—the Chorus group to either side

Yet, there came a night of great change ... There was a dispute, it was
said, between two bucks.

Two Bucks enter wearing full head-masks

Buck 1 Justice, O First of the Tigers!
Buck 2 Judgment, O Judge of the Jungle!
Tiger What is the dispute?
Buck 1 He invades my grazing!
Buck 2 He steals my wives!
Buck 1 Thou liest!
Buck 2 Thou liest, thou hornless fawn!!

The Bucks fight

Tiger Silence!

The Bucks fall silent

How has he invaded your grazing?
Buck 1 The stream, O Judge, is the border of my grazing-land. He crossed it
to feed.
Buck 2 Because he crossed it to steal my does!

The Bucks fight

Tiger Silence!

The Bucks fall silent

How many does has he stolen?

Buck 2 Two, O Judge! Two of the youngest.
Buck 1 None, O Judge. They were mine from the first!
Buck 2 Thou liest!
Buck 1 Thou liest, thou double-tongued worm!!

They fight

Tiger Silence!

Nothing

  Silence!

Nothing

  SILENCE!!

Tiger strikes Buck and kills it

Hathi Till that night none of us had died, and the First of the Tigers, seeing what he had done and being made foolish by the scent of blood, ran away into the marshes of the North.

Tha enters

Tha What is this? Where is the First of the Tigers? Who killed?
Hathi Then some said this and some said that but the scent of blood made us foolish and we could not say who had killed.
Tha Then hear me, O trees that hang low and trailing creepers of the Jungle. When the killer of the buck runs by you, do you mark him with your branches and your tendrils. (*To the others*) As for you . . . you have shown that ye cannot keep the Law. Therefore ye must have another Law and a Law that ye cannot break. Now shall ye know Fear, and when ye have found him ye shall know that he is your master and the rest shall follow.
Wolf What is Fear?
Tha Seek and ye shall find.

The animals search. A pipe is heard

  Into their midst walks a Man

They look. He laughs. They hide. When their faces re-emerge from behind their "trees" the peaceful, idealized masks have gone and their faces are full of savagery and fear. The Man shouts. The animals flee

Hathi When the First of the Tigers heard about Fear he left his hiding-place.
Tiger I will go to this thing and break its neck.

Tiger sets off. The Chorus as creepers paint stripes upon him as he goes. Tiger finds Man. Man laughs

Man What is this striped one that comes by night? Ha!!

Tiger flees. He tries to rub off the stripes. He comes across other animals. They flee. Tha emerges

Tiger O Tha, why is it that I am become striped and that I fear the Hairless
One and that the Jungle People fear me?

Tha Thou hast killed the buck. Thou hast let Death loose in the Jungle, and
with Death has come Fear, so that the People of the Jungle are afraid of
thee as thou art afraid of the Hairless One. (*Tha turns to go*)

Tiger Do not go! Do not forget me, O Tha! Remember that I was once the
Master of the Jungle. Let my children remember that I was once without
shame or Fear.

Tha This much will I do, because thou and I together saw the Jungle being
made. For one night in each year it shall be as it was before the buck was
killed—for thee and thy children. In that one Night, if ye meet the
Hairless One—and his name is Man—ye shall not be afraid of him, but he
shall be afraid of thee. Show him mercy in that night of his fear, for thou
hast known what fear is.

Tiger I am content.

Hathi But when next he drank, the Tiger saw the stripes upon his flank and
hide and he remembered the name that the Hairless One had called him,
and he was angry. For a year he lived in the marshes until Tha should keep
his promise. And upon a night when the Jackal of the Moon stood
clear of the Jungle, he felt that his Night was on him and he went to the
cave to meet the Hairless One.

*The spot on Hathi fades. Tiger comes to Man. Man is frightened. Tiger kills
him. Thunder*

Tha Is this thy mercy?

Tiger What matter? Fear is now as the buck was. His back is broken. Let all
the Jungle know that I have killed Fear.

Tha Thou hast untied the feet of Death, and he will follow thee till thou
diest. Thou hast taught Man to kill.

The Man's corpse laughs. Then another laugh is heard. Then another

Men appear from all directions armed with spears

*Their laughter becomes a shout as they thrust at the Tiger. Thunder. Black-
out. The mythical scene vanishes. The Lights come up on Hathi and Mowgli*

Younger Mowgli On one night only does Man fear the tiger?

Hathi For one night only. On other nights, if Shere Khan kills Man he
springs from behind. But on his Night he goes down into the village and
looks Man in the eye and the men fall on their faces and he kills.

Younger Mowgli Now I see why it was Shere Khan bade me look at him. He
got no good of it, for he could not hold his eyes steady and I did not fall
down at his feet. But then I am not a man, being of the Free People.

*Thunder. Rain. Reactions. The Lights come up on the lower level—bright
daylight*

Bagheera Aaah! The cloud breaks and the rains come! We shall see the
Mowha in blossom yet, eh Baloo? And the little fawns all fat with grass!

Deer etc. The Truce! The Truce still holds!!

Hathi Let the Truce hold for this night, that each may drink his fill without fear. Honour the Truce, Bagheera.

Bagheera I jest, O Hathi! I break no Truces. I am no creeper-striped man-eater.

Younger Mowgli Aieeya! The water! Feel the rain! My skin drinks. Was this not worth the wait, Baloo?

Baloo Ay, Little Frog. Well worth the wait. Worth the little food and the less drink and the bones showing through the flesh. Come out now, for it is time for thy lessons.

Younger Mowgli My lessons and thy bath, Old Bear! (*He splashes Baloo*)

Baloo Waugh! So it is bath-time is it? (*He pushes Mowgli's face under the water*) Well that will do to start with. Remember:

> His spots are the joy of the leopard; his horns are the buffalo's pride.
> Be clean, for the strength of a hunter is known by the gloss of his hide.

Repeat!

The other animals fade away

Bagheera lies on the upper level upstage

SCENE 6

Younger Mowgli	His spots are the joy of the leopard; his horns are the buffalo's pride.
	Be clean for the . . .
Baloo	Strength of a hunter . . .
Younger Mowgli	I know!
	. . . the strength of a hunter is known by the gloss of his hide.
	There, am I not thy best pupil?
Baloo	"There is none like to me", says the cub, in the pride of his earliest kill,
	But the Jungle is large and the cub he is small, let him think—and be still.
	Repeat!

Mowgli repeats it

The Stranger's hunting call?

Younger Mowgli (*looking around*) "Give me leave to hunt because I am hungry."

Baloo And the answer?

Younger Mowgli "Hunt then for food, but not for pleasure." (*Finding the pipe he has been searching for*) See, Baloo, I can play on a pipe like the men do. (*He plays the "invisible" pipe*)

Baloo What do you say to Mang the Bat when you disturb him in the branches by day?

Younger Mowgli "Pardon, Brother, for breaking your rest. May you have good hunting this night." I made the pipe from a reed.

Baloo The hunting verse of the Free People?

Younger Mowgli "Feet that make no noise; eyes that can see in the dark; ears that can hear the winds in their lairs . . ." Oh I have said it a world of times. I shall play your tune no longer, Baloo, I have my own tune to play.

Baloo knocks him off his feet with a blow of his paw

Owww! My head sings! I'll have no more of you Old Blind One! Let the man come and send the stinging fly that comes out of his white smoke and use your hide to cover him on cold nights!

Mowgli runs off

Bagheera (*who has been observing this*) What is this, Old Bear? Must you forever beat the brains out of your best pupil?

Baloo Best pupil? Ay, he learns fast but he is wilder than the cubs of an Outlier! He has just wished my hide to be taken by a man!

Bagheera You keep him at lessons too long! The wolf-cubs you let go when they know the Hunting Verse.

Baloo Pah! Have I not told you that a man's cub is a man's cub and must know all the Laws of the Jungle?

Bagheera But think how small he is. How can his little head carry all thy long talk?

Baloo Is there anything in the Jungle too little to be killed? That is why I teach him these things, and that is why I hit him, very softly, when he forgets.

Bagheera Softly! What does thou know of softness, Old Iron-feet? His face is always bruised from thy softness.

Baloo Better that he should be bruised from head to foot by me who love him than that he should come to harm through ignorance. I am now teaching him the Master-words so that he can claim protection, if he will only remember them, from the birds and the snake people and all in the Jungle. Is that not worth a little beating?

Bagheera The Master-words? I should like to know more of those.

Baloo I will call Mowgli and he shall say them—if he will. Come little brother!—Mowgli!

Mowgli appears from an unexpected direction, creeps up behind Baloo, blows the pipe loudly in his ear, then runs to Bagheera

Younger Mowgli My head is ringing like a bee-tree. I come for Bagheera and not for thee, fat, old Baloo!

Baloo That is all one to me. Tell Bagheera, then, the Master-words of the Jungle that I have taught thee this day.

Younger Mowgli Master-words for which people? The Jungle has many tongues. I know them all.

Baloo A little thou knowest, but not much. Say the word for the Hunting-People, then—great scholar.

Younger Mowgli We be of one blood, ye and I.

Baloo Good. Now for the birds.

Younger Mowgli We be of one blood, ye and I. (*He whistles like a kite*)

Bagheera Now for the Snake-People.

Younger Mowgli (*in a snake-voice*) We be of one blood, ye and I.

Mowgli hisses enthusiastically, applauds and jumps on to Bagheera's back

Baloo There, there! That was worth a little bruise. Some day thou wilt remember me.

Bagheera Thy knowledge is great, Old Teacher. I knew nothing of the Master-words of the other folk.

Baloo Nor I, Old Hunter. But Hathi, the Elephant, knows all such things. I begged them from him.

Younger Mowgli Just now I spoke with the grey apes ...

Bagheera Even the Snake-People!

Baloo Ah! That Hathi knew but could not speak. Nor I ...

Younger Mowgli They had heard of my wisdom and knowledge ...

Baloo Hathi came with Mowgli and me and we went to the shallow pools to ask the Water-Snake ...

Younger Mowgli They wish to make me their King ...

Baloo And the man-cub learnt the Word from the Water-Snake's mouth!

Younger Mowgli And so I shall have a tribe of my own and lead them through the Jungle all day long.

Bagheera What is this new folly, little dreamer of dreams?

Younger Mowgli Yes, and throw branches and dirt at old Baloo. They have promised me this. Ah!

Baloo knocks him over and pins him to the ground

Baloo Mowgli, thou hast been talking with the Monkey-People.

Mowgli looks at Bagheera for support

Bagheera Thou hast been with the Monkey-People—the grey apes—the people without a Law—the eaters of everything. That is great shame.

Younger Mowgli When Baloo hurt my head I went away, and the grey apes came down from the trees and had pity on me.

Baloo The pity of the Monkey-People!! The stillness of the mountain stream! The coolness of the summer sun! And then, Man-cub?

Younger Mowgli And then they gave me nuts and pleasant things to eat and said I was their blood-brother and should be their leader some day.

Bagheera They have no leader. They lie. They have always lied.

Younger Mowgli They were very kind and bade me come again. Why have I never been taken among the Monkey-People? They stand on their feet as I do. They do not hit me with hard paws. They play all day. Let me get up! Bad Baloo, let me up! I will play with them again.

Baloo Listen, Man-cub; I have taught thee all the Law of the Jungle for all the peoples of the Jungle—except the Monkey-Folk. They have no Law. They are outcasts. They have no speech of their own, but use the stolen words they overhear when they listen, and peep, and wait up above in the branches. Their way is not our way. They are without leaders. They have no remembrance. They boast and chatter and pretend that they are a great people about to do great affairs in the Jungle, but the falling of a nut turns their minds to laughter and all is forgotten. We of the Jungle have no dealings with them. We do not drink where the monkeys drink; we do not go where the monkeys go; we do not hunt where they hunt; we do not die where they die. Hast thou ever heard me speak of the Bandar-Log until today?

Younger Mowgli (*whispering*) No.

The Jungle has fallen unnaturally silent

Baloo The Jungle-People put them out of their mouths and out of their minds. They are very many, evil, dirty, shameless, and they desire, if they have any fixed desire, to be noticed by the Jungle-People.

During this speech angry noises grow in the tree-tops, culminating in a shower of nuts, twigs and leaves being thrown at the animals below

But we do not notice them, even when they throw nuts and filth on our heads. The Monkey-People are forbidden—forbidden to the Jungle-People. Remember.

Bagheera Forbidden. But I still think Baloo should have warned thee against them.

Baloo I? How was I to guess he would play with such dirt? The Monkey-People! Faugh!

Renewed imprecations and missiles from above

Younger Mowgli They can hear you. They are angry.

Baloo Their anger is as unreal as their pity. Pay no attention to them. They will soon weary of the game.

Bagheera The sun is high. It is time to sleep, Little Brother.

Bagheera and Baloo stretch out for sleep. Mowgli looks on. The monkey noises die

Baloo There. Did I not say they would tire quickly. Such is the way of all their kind. Sleep, now, Little Frog. Another lesson is learned.

Bagheera and Baloo sleep. Mowgli settles down under a "tree". Long pause. Gradually, infinitesimally, we hear monkey sounds. Mowgli looks around to see where they are coming from. Suddenly he is yanked into the tree

Younger Mowgli Baloo! Bagheera!

Great noise of triumphant monkeys. Baloo and Bagheera wake

Baloo Aah! What nonsense now?

Bagheera Mowgli.

Baloo Mowgli? Little Brother, where are you?

Younger Mowgli Baloo!!

Monkey Look up, Baloo! Look up, Bagheera, and admire the skill and cunning of the Bandar-Log! We have your man-cub. Now catch us. If you can.

The Monkeys retreat with Mowgli

Baloo and Bagheera try to spot them in the trees

Baloo Mowgli!!

Bagheera Why didst thou not warn the man-cub? What was the use of half-slaying him with blows if thou didst not warn him?

Baloo Haste! Oh, haste! We—we may catch them yet!

Bagheera At your speed? It would not tire a wounded cow. Sit still and think! Make a plan. This is no time for chasing. They may drop him if we follow too close.

Baloo stops shuffling up and down

Baloo They may have dropped him already, being tired of carrying him. Arula! Whoo! Put dead bats on my head! Roll me in the hives of the wild bees that I may be stung to death and bury me with the Hyena! O Mowgli, Mowgli! Why did I not warn thee against the Monkey-Folk?

Bagheera Baloo, thou art utterly lacking in pride. What would the Jungle think if I curled myself up like Ikki the Porcupine and howled?

Baloo What do I care what the Jungle thinks? He may be dead by now!

Bagheera Unless they drop him in sport or kill him out of idleness I have no fear of the man-cub. He is wise and well-taught and above all he has the eyes that make the Jungle People afraid. But he is in the power of the Bandar-Log and because they live in the trees they have no fear of any of our people.

Baloo Fool that I am! Oh, fat, brown, root-digging fool that I am. The Monkey-Folk fear Kaa, the rock-snake. He can climb as well as they and he steals the young monkeys in the night. The whisper of his name makes their wicked tails turn cold. Let us go to Kaa.

Bagheera What will he do for us? He is not of our tribe—being footless and with most evil eyes.

Baloo He is very old and cunning. Above all he is very hungry. Promise him many goats. It must be Kaa. Kaa is our only hope.

Kaa appears above them

Kaa Do I hear one speak my name?

Baloo It is he! Good hunting, Kaa. That is a fine new skin thou hast!

Kaa Good hunting to us all!! Come closer, friend, that I may see who thou art.

Bagheera (*whispering*) Take care, Old Bear. He is always quick to strike after he has changed his skin.

Baloo Ay, but also at this time he does not see well. The risk must be taken. Greetings, Kaa. It is I, Baloo.

Kaa Oho, Baloo, what dost thou here? And Bagheera is it not? Is there news of game afoot. I am empty as a dried well.

Baloo We are hunting.

Kaa Let me come with you. A blow more or less is nothing to hunters such as you, but I, I have to wait for days in a wood-path and climb half the night on the mere chance of a young ape. (*He hisses*) The branches are not what they were when I was young. I came near to falling on my last hunt, and the noise of my slipping waked the Bandar-Log and they called me the most evil names.

Bagheera (*murmuring*) "Worm".

Kaa Ssss! Have they called me that?

Bagheera Ah, yes. "Footless, yellow, earth-worm." That was it. But they will say anything——

Kaa The Bandar-Log have shifted their grounds. I heard them whooping among the tree-tops.

Baloo It is the Bandar-Log we follow now ...

Kaa The Bandar-Log! Two such great hunters?

Bagheera Ay. Those nut-stealers and pickers of palm-leaves have stolen our man-cub, of whom thou hast perhaps heard.

Baloo Therefore we came to you for we know that of all the Jungle People they fear Kaa alone.

Kaa They have good reason. They call me also—yellow fish was it not?

Bagheera Worm.

Baloo Worm.

Bagheera Yellow worm.

Baloo Yellow worm.

Bagheera Yellow earth-worm ...

Baloo Yellow ...

Kaa (*hissing*) We must remind them to speak well of their master. We must help their wandering memories. Now, whither went they with the man-cub?

Baloo The Jungle alone knows. Toward the sunset I believe. We thought that thou wouldst know, O Kaa.

Kaa I? How? I take them when they come my way, but I do not hunt the Bandar-Log, or frogs—or green scum on a water-hole for that matter.

Chil appears above

Chil Up, up! Look up Baloo of the Seonee Wolf-Pack!

Baloo Who is it?

Bagheera It is Chil the Kite. Speak, Chil. What news?

Chil I have seen the man-cub among the Bandar-Log. He bade me tell you. The Bandar-Log have taken him to their monkey-city—to the Cold Lairs. They may stay there a night, or ten nights, or an hour. I have told the bats to watch through the dark-time. That is my message. Good hunting!

Bagheera Full gorge and deep sleep to you, Chil. I will remember thee in my next kill and set aside the head for thee alone, O best of Kites.

Chil It is nothing. The boy held the Master-word. I could have done no less.

Baloo He has not forgotten to use his tongue. To think of one so young remembering the Master-Word for the birds while he was being pulled through the trees.

Bagheera It was most firmly driven into him. But I am proud of him. And now for our journey. It will take us half the night—at full speed.

Baloo I will go as fast as I can.

Bagheera We dare not wait for thee. Follow. We must go on the quick-foot, Kaa and I.

Kaa Feet or no feet, I can keep abreast of all thy four. However, there will be climbing to do when we arrive and I am slow to climb.

Bagheera Then for a time it may be that I shall fight alone. But for now let us make haste to the Cold Lairs.

Tableau. Chord. Black-out. Fast sitar music into the next scene

> SCENE 7

Gisborne's verandah on the upper level

Older Mowgli The Cold Lairs was an old, deserted city, lost and buried in the Jungle, and beasts seldom use a place that man has used. Ha! My story is too long for the Sahib.

Gisborne Too long? No, it's splendid. I'm just a little tired, Mowgli, that's all.

Older Mowgli Well, the talking has done me good. Farewell, Sahib.

Gisborne Wait! Will you come back? Another night? Or to work?

Older Mowgli To work? Ah, Sahib, I think I have no need of money, or . . . what was that other thing? A pension, whatever that may be. But perhaps another night I shall wish to talk. Farewell, Sahib. Do not let that old rogue, your servant, rob you.

Mowgli retires from the main area but does not exit

Gisborne Abdul!

Abdul emerges from behind the curtain

Abdul Sahib?

Gisborne I'll go to bed, now, Abdul.

Abdul He is gone, that gipsy?

Gisborne Yes, back into the Jungle.

Abdul Come, Sahib, it is late.

They go out, Gisborne taking the bottle, Abdul taking the gun and clapping his hands and calling "Amira!"

Amira, Abdul's daughter comes in to clear the table

Mowgli steps into silhouette, watching. The girl finds Gisborne's glass, checks that her father is busy off, lowers her veil and tastes the drink. Mowgli laughs

Amira gasps, pulls up her veil and runs off

Older Mowgli It is in my mind that perhaps this is what is meant by a pension! Perhaps, after all, I shall serve Queen Victoria.

The Lights fade to Black-out

ACT II

SCENE 1

Gisborne's verandah. Night

Abdul rushes on to the verandah and starts to load the gun

Abdul Up! Up Sahib!
Gisborne (*off*) What the devil? Abdul . . .?
Abdul Up Sahib! Up and take thy gun. Mine honour is gone. Up and kill before any see.
Gisborne (*off*) Have you gone mad, Abdul?

Gisborne enters, hitching up his trousers

Abdul (*muttering*) It was for this, then, that that jungle outcast helped me to polish the Sahib's table and drew water and plucked fowls.
Gisborne What are you talking about? Give me that gun.
Abdul They have gone off together for all my beatings, and now he sits among his devils dragging her soul to the pit.
Gisborne Mowgli?
Abdul And my daughter, my Amira. Oh shame! Shame! They are out there in the forest. Come we shall find them and kill.
Gisborne Wait! If Mowgli has run off with your daughter then he has wronged you, and I shall help you—within the law. But there will be no killing. Can you wonder that she went to him after all your beatings!
Abdul Come, Sahib and bring thy gun. He may have his devils with him.

Abdul draws his dagger and exits. Gisborne follows

Black-out

SCENE 2

The Jungle

Black-out. The sound of a flute is heard in the Jungle. After a few seconds, the Lights come up on the lower level. Moonlight

Mowgli is seated playing. Amira lies, resting her head against his thigh. Silence

Amira My father says thou art a magician. Art thou human-born to play such music?
Older Mowgli Indeed I am human-born. I know that because my heart is in

thy hold, Little One. But I was a wolf among wolves none the less till a time came when those of the Jungle bade me go because I was a man.
Amira Who bade thee go?
Older Mowgli The very beasts themselves. Then I went down to the village and was a herder of cattle.
Amira To the village? And where was thy heart then? Thou hast seen other maids in the village, maids fairer than I; I—that am a maid no more—have I thy heart?
Older Mowgli What shall I swear by? By Allah, of whom thou speakest?
Amira Nay, by the life that is in thee, and I am well content, but how can I believe thy vows when a child would not believe thy tales?
Older Mowgli What tales?
Amira Thy tale to the Englishman, I heard it all through the curtain. Arré, thou art a wondrous liar my lover.
Older Mowgli By the Bull that bought me, all I said that night was true.
Amira Of thy capture by the Monkey-Folk?
Older Mowgli And my rescue!! ... Shh! (*He listens*) Ha! Thy father hath discovered his loss. He and Gisborne Sahib are tracking us through the jungle.

Amira moves

Have no fear. It will take them time enough to find this place. When they come we will be gone. But for now, rest easy, Little One. Believe my words and I shall tell thee my story. When the Monkey-People captured me they swung me through the tree tops, high and dizzy, till I had no sense of where I was or in what direction I was going. By good fortune, Chil the Kite, saw them, and knew they were taking me to the Cold Lairs.

Sitar chord. The Lights fade on Mowgli and Amira

SCENE 3

The Cold Lairs. Lower level

A spot hits the first Narrator. The lighting then widens to include others as they speak. As each Narrator finishes speaking, he joins the growing band of Monkeys pantomiming the actions described in the speech

Narrator The Cold Lairs was an old, deserted city, lost and buried in the Jungle, and beasts seldom use a place that Man has once used./Besides the grey apes lived there as much as they could be said to live anywhere and no self-respecting animal would come within eyeshot of it, except in times of drought when the half-ruined tanks and reservoirs held a little water./ Some king had built the city long ago on a little hill. From the palace you could see the rows and rows of roofless houses looking like empty honeycombs filled with blackness./The monkeys called the place their city, and pretended to despise the Jungle People because they lived in the forest. And yet they never knew what the buildings were made for or how to use them./They would sit in circles in the hall of the king's council-chamber, and scratch for fleas and pretend to be men./They drank at the tanks and made the water all muddy, and then they fought over it, and then they would all rush together in mobs and shout/"There is no-one in the Jungle so wise and good and clever and strong as the Bandar-Log."

The Monkeys drift away

Then all would begin again until they grew tired of their city and went back to the tree-tops, hoping the Jungle-People would notice them./

Head Monkey appears. He beckons the Narrator

On the day they captured Mowgli they were feeling particularly pleased with themselves . . .

The Lights come up to daylight. The Narrator joins the Monkeys

The Monkeys' entrances should be as acrobatic as possible. As they sing, some carry on Younger Mowgli, others leap and tumble. During the song they quarrel and fight, but always get distracted before they express their grandiose intentions

The Road-Song of the Bandar-Log

Monkeys   Here we go in a flung festoon
             Half-way up to the jealous moon.
             Don't you envy our pranceful bands?
             Don't you wish you had extra hands?
             Wouldn't you like if your tails were so—
             Curved in the shape of a Cupid's Bow?
             Now we're going to—never mind!
             Brother, thy tail hangs down behind!

             Here we sit in a branchy row,
             Thinking of beautiful things we know;
             Dreaming of deeds we mean to do,
             All complete in a minute or two—
             Something noble and grand and good
             Won by merely wishing we could.
             Now we're going to—never mind!
             Brother, thy tail hangs down behind!

             All the talk we ever have heard
             Uttered by bat or beast or bird—
             Hide or fin or scale or feather—
             Jabber it quickly and all together!
             Excellent! Wonderful! Once again!
             Now we are talking just like men.
             Let's pretend we're . . . never mind,
             Brother thy tail hangs down behind!
             This is the way of the Monkey-kind.

Monkey 1 Welcome, Man-cub, to the great city of the Bandar-Log.

Monkey 2 The wise, the great, the most beautiful people of the Jungle!

Monkey 1 The coming of the man-cub, my Brothers, marks a new ... thing in the history of the Bandar-Log ...

Noisy Monkey The man-cub will teach us to weave sticks together ...

Monkey 1 (*after beating up Noisy Monkey*) The man-cub will teach us to weave sticks together to shield us from the rain and cold. We shall be the greatest of the Jungle People.

Monkey 2 We are already the greatest of the Jungle People.

Noisy Monkey We shall become like men! The man-cub will teach us how to use the red flower.

Monkey 1 again beats him up, then goes to drink at the tank

Monkey 2 We are great. We are wise. We are free.

Monkey 4 We are wonderful!

Monkey 5 The most wonderful people in all the Jungle.

Monkey 6 We all say so, so it must be true.

Monkey 1 (*to Mowgli*) Now ...

Too much noise. Monkey 1 beats up a few Monkeys

Now ...

Noisy Monkey is still making a noise. Monkey 1 and the others near him beat him up. He flees to his mother who faces off Monkey 1 and co

Now, Man-cub, as you are a new listener and can carry our words back to the Jungle People so that they may notice us in future, we shall tell you all about ourselves ...

Monkey 2 Yes, all about the clever, wise and gentle Bandar-Log.

The Monkeys start to chatter all together. Some break into their song

Bagheera (*off*) Bagheera!!!

The Monkeys freeze, then scatter as ...

Bagheera leaps into their midst

By the time he and Mowgli are face to face the only Monkey to be seen is Monkey 1, who cowers in a corner. He looks up and sees Bagheera

Monkey 1 There is only one here! Kill him! Kill him!

Monkey 2 Hide the man-cub!

Mowgli is put under guard. Bagheera fights the Monkeys but is soon buried under them. Mowgli yells

Younger Mowgli To the tank, Bagheera! Roll and plunge! Roll to the water-tank. They will not follow thee into the water!

Bagheera works his way to the water-tank. He plunges in. Monkeys line along the edge of the tank, screaming. Bagheera splashes them

Baloo (*off*) I come, Bagheera! Baloo is here!

Baloo enters

Big fight. Monkeys flying through the air, being thrown, climbing on Baloo, being swept aside by his paws. Eventually they bury him beneath them. Some remain guarding Bagheera

Bagheera Kaa! Where are you, Kaa? We have need of you!!

At the name of Kaa the Monkeys fall silent

Kaa enters

Kaa Have patience. I am come.
Monkeys Kaa! It is Kaa! Run! Run! (*They turn to run*)
Kaa Sssssstay!

The Monkeys freeze

Look at me.

They do

Ssstay you sso! (*To Bagheera*) I could not come before, Brother, but I think I heard thee call.
Bagheera I—I may have cried out in the heat of the battle. Baloo, art thou hurt!
Baloo I am sore enough. But it is nothing. See, see the man-cub is safe. Art thou hurt, Little Brother?

Mowgli has released himself from his hypnotized captors and comes over to the others

Younger Mowgli I am sore and hungry and bruised. But oh, they have handled ye grievously, my Brothers! Ye bleed.
Bagheera Others also.
Kaa So this is the manling. Very soft is his skin and he is not so unlike the Bandar-Log. Have a care, Manling, that I do not mistake thee for a monkey, some twilight when I have newly changed my coat.
Younger Mowgli We be of one blood, thou and I. (*He hisses*) I take my life from thee tonight. My kill shall be thy kill if ever thou art hungry, O Kaa.
Baloo Well said.
Kaa A brave heart and a courteous tongue. They shall carry thee far through the Jungle, Manling. But now go hence quickly with thy friends—what follows it is not well thou shouldst see. Bandar-Log. Can ye stir foot or hand without my order? Speak.
Monkeys Without thy order we cannot stir hand or foot, O Kaa.
Kaa Look at me. Look at my eyes.

Kaa sways to and fro, looking at each Monkey in turn. The others watch, fascinated. The sway turns into a hypnotic dance which virtually becomes a dance of seduction. Finally the Monkeys are in thrall and Kaa is still

Bandar-Log. Come all one pace closer to me.

They do so, as do Baloo and Bagheera

Closer.
Younger Mowgli Baloo! Bagheera! Come away.

Mowgli, Baloo and Bagheera turn away and move off. In the background the Monkeys move closer to Kaa. When they are in as tight a group as possible, they freeze

Bagheera Keep thy hand on my shoulder. Keep it there or I must go to Kaa.
Baloo Whoof! Never more will I make an ally of Kaa!
Bagheera In a little time, had I stayed, I should have walked down his throat.
Baloo Many will walk that road before the moon rises again.
Younger Mowgli But what was the meaning of it all? I saw nothing but a big snake swaying to and fro.
Bagheera Mowgli! He put himself into danger on thy account, just as my ears and sides and paws and Baloo's neck and shoulders are bitten on thy account. Neither Baloo nor Bagheera will be able to hunt with pleasure for many days.
Baloo It is nothing. We have the man-cub again.
Bagheera True, but it has cost us heavily in time, in hair—I am plucked all along my back—and last of all in honour. For remember, Mowgli, I who am the Black Panther, was forced to call on Kaa for protection. All this, Man-cub, came of thy playing with the Bandar-Log.
Younger Mowgli True. It is true. I am an evil man-cub and my stomach is sad within me.
Bagheera What says the Law of the Jungle, Baloo?
Baloo "Sorrow never stays punishment." But remember he is very little.
Bagheera I will remember. But he has done mischief and blows must be dealt. Mowgli, hast thou anything to say?
Younger Mowgli Nothing. I did wrong. Baloo and thou are wounded. It is just.

Bagheera clips him, sending him sprawling. Baloo, reluctantly, does the same. Mowgli sneezes, picks himself up

Baloo Now jump on my shoulder, Little Brother, and we will go home.

Tableau. Sitar chord. The Lights fade to Black-out

SCENE 4

A spot comes up on the Narrator

Narrator It was one very warm day that a new notion came to Bagheera—born of something that he had heard. Late afternoon, when they were deep in the Jungle, he said to Mowgli——

The Lights come up—warm daylight

Bagheera Little Brother, how often have I told thee that Shere Khan is thy enemy?

Younger Mowgli As many times as there are nuts on that palm. What of it? I am sleepy, Bagheera, and Shere Khan is all long tail and loud talk—like Mao, the Peacock.

Bagheera Tabaqui has told thee too.

Younger Mowgli (*laughing*) Tabaqui came to me not long ago with some rude talk that I was a naked man's cub and not fit to dig pig-nuts; but I caught Tabaqui by the tail and swung him twice against a palm-tree to teach him better manners.

Bagheera That was foolishness: for though Tabaqui is a mischief-maker, he would have told thee of something that concerned thee closely. Open those eyes, Little Brother; Shere Khan dare not kill thee in the Jungle, but he has taught many of the young wolves that a man-cub has no place in the Pack. In a little time thou wilt be a man.

Younger Mowgli And what is a man that he should not run with his brothers? I was born in the Jungle. I have obeyed the Law of the Jungle, and there is no wolf of ours from whose paws I have not pulled a thorn. Surely they are my brothers!

Bagheera Little Brother, feel under my jaw.

Mowgli does so

You feel it? The small, hairless patch. There is no-one in the Jungle besides thee that knows that I, Bagheera, carry that mark—the mark of the collar; and yet, Little Brother, I was born among men, and it was among men that my mother died—in the cages of the King's Palace at Oodeypore. It was because of this that I paid the price for thee at the Council when thou wast a little, naked cub. Yes, I too was born among men. I had never seen the Jungle. They fed me behind iron bars from an iron pan until one night I felt that I was Bagheera—and no man's plaything—and I broke the silly lock with a blow of my paw and came away; and because I had learned the ways of men I became more terrible in the Jungle than Shere Khan. Is it not so?

Younger Mowgli Yes. All the Jungle fear Bagheera—all except Mowgli.

Bagheera Oh, *thou* art a man's cub, and even as I returned to the Jungle, so thou must go back to men at last—to the men who are thy brothers—if thou art not killed in the Council.

Younger Mowgli But why—but why should anyone wish to kill me?

Bagheera Look at me.

Mowgli does so. After a long pause, Bagheera turns away

That is why. Not even I can look thee between the eyes, and I was born among men, and I love thee, Little Brother. The others they hate thee because their eyes cannot meet thine—because thou art wise—because thou hast pulled thorns from their feet—because thou art a man.

Younger Mowgli I did not know these things.

Bagheera What is the Law of the Jungle? "Strike first and then give tongue." By thy very carelessness they know thou art a man. It is in my heart that Akela is getting old and will soon miss his kill. When that happens the Pack will turn against thee. Shere Khan has told the wolves to bring Akela up against a strong, untried buck tonight to make his weakness known. When he misses his kill he will no longer be Leader and you will have lost a protector.

Younger Mowgli But I have thee, Bagheera, and Baloo . . .

Bagheera We cannot be with thee all the time, Mowgli.

Younger Mowgli And Grey Brother . . .

Bagheera And Grey Brother, though he would defend thee to the death, is but one wolf against many. And Shere Khan . . .

Younger Mowgli Shere Khan is an eater of frogs . . .

Bagheera Though an eater of frogs, is yet a tiger with a tiger's strength . . . Mowgli, pay heed to Bagheera! There is a time for attack and a time for cunning. Thou art not yet strong enough to face Shere Khan. Thou art still a cub—a man's cub—but even so a cub.

Younger Mowgli Then what must I do?

Bagheera Go now. Leave the Jungle. Go to Man. Learn Man's cunning; learn to use his weapons; learn to speak his language, grow amongst men. Then, when next you come . . .

Younger Mowgli When next I come to the Council Rock it will be with Shere Khan's hide on my head.

Bagheera Thou art a man indeed.

Younger Mowgli But first I must say farewell to my mother, and Baloo and . . .

Bagheera Look around, Little Brother. They are come.

Mother Wolf, Father Wolf, Baloo, Grey Brother enter

Younger Mowgli They knew?

Bagheera They knew. You only were blind to it all. But say farewell quickly for they must soon join the hunt. Akela will need his friends tonight.

Mowgli starts to cry

Younger Mowgli What is this? What is it? I do not wish to leave the Jungle and I do not know what is this water from my eyes. Am I dying, Bagheera?

Bagheera No, Little Brother. These are only tears such as men use.

Baloo Tears? I have heard of such things. Let them fall, Mowgli. They do no harm.

Younger Mowgli Grey Brother, you will not forget me?

Grey Brother Never while I can follow a trail. Come to the foot of the hill when thou art a man and I will talk to thee; and I will come into the croplands to play with thee by night.

Baloo Come soon, O best of pupils, for thy teacher grows old and his eyes are dim.

Father Wolf Come soon, little naked son of mine.

Mother Wolf Come soon O thou Mowgli; for listen, child of man, I loved thee more than ever I loved my cubs.

Younger Mowgli I will surely come, and when I come it will be with Shere Khan's hide. Do not forget me! Tell them in the Jungle never to forget me!

Mowgli leaves

Bagheera That is a man. That is all a man. O Shere Khan, never was a blacker hunting than that frog-hunt of thine ten years ago.

Tableau. Sitar chord. The Lights fade to Black-out

SCENE 5

A Jungle Path

The cast stand upstage to L *and* R. *A spot comes up on the Narrator*

Younger Mowgli runs on, stops C *and drinks*

Narrator Mowgli was far and far through the Jungle and his heart was hot within him.

Dim green lighting comes up on Mowgli

As the evening mist rose he came to the stream at the bottom of the valley. There he checked for he heard the sound of the wolf-pack hunting.

Howls of Wolves mingled with shouts. "Akela! Akela! Let the lone wolf show his strength. Room for the leader of the Pack! Spring, Akela!" Sound of Akela's snarl. Silence. A dismal howl. "He has missed! Akela has missed the kill! Call the Council! To the Council Rock! The man-cub! Where is the man-cub!" The Pack settle down to a steady purposeful chant of "Man-cub, man-cub, man-cub." The drum joins them

Younger Mowgli Bagheera spoke truth.

Mowgli starts to run. Heartbeat. In the following chorus piece a fast, exciting beat is set. Disco-type lighting, tied to drumbeat, on Mowgli as his running becomes more and more of a headlong dash. The voices start low and muted, ending up high and loud. The Lighting on the Chorus upstage of Mowgli is just on the faces with torches as in the first piece of verse in Act I, Scene 1

Chorus   E'er Mao the Peacock flutters, e'er the Monkey People cry
                E'er Chil the Kite swoops down a furlong sheer,
                Through the Jungle very softly flits a shadow and a sigh—
                He is Fear, O Little Hunter, he is Fear!
                Very softly down the glade runs a waiting, watching shade,
                And the whisper spreads and widens far and near;
                And the sweat is on thy brow, for he passes even now—
                He is Fear, O Little Hunter, he is Fear!

                E'er the moon has climbed the mountain, e'er the rocks are
                     ribbed with light,
                When the downward-dipping trails are dank and drear,
                Comes a breathing hard behind thee—snuffle-snuffle
                     through the night.
                It is Fear, O Little Hunter, it is Fear!
                On thy knees and draw the bow; bid the shrilling arrow go;

> In the empty, mocking thicket plunge the spear;
> But thy hands are loosed and weak, and the blood has left
>   thy cheek—
> It is Fear, O Little Hunter, it is Fear!

The Chorus repeat "Fear, Fear" in whispers as Faces vanish. One face remains. Heartbeat

Face Now thy throat is shut and dried, and thy heart against thy side Hammers: Fear, O Little Hunter—this is Fear!

The Face vanishes

Mowgli waits at the forest edge, getting his breath back. He moves as if to part the branches at the forest edge. Broad daylight comes up. He steps out of the Jungle. A dog barks. He walks towards it. Sounds of cattle. A baby cries. A mother sings to it. Mowgli nears the village. A Man is hoeing the crop, his food wrapped in a cloth at his side. Mowgli watches him

The Man turns, sees Mowgli and runs off with a cry of "Buldeo!"

Mowgli shrugs and inspects the Man's food. He tries some. It is highly-flavoured. He tries it again and starts to enjoy it

A Young Girl dashes on, then Buldeo with his gun, then the other Villagers. Buldeo approaches Mowgli

Mowgli snarls at him and snaps. Buldeo withdraws

Priest What is there to be afraid of? Look at the marks on his arms and legs. They are the bites of wolves. He is but a wolf-child run away from the Jungle.

Messua Arre! Arre! To be bitten by wolves, poor child!

Young Girl He is a handsome boy.

2nd Girl He has eyes like red fire.

Woman By mine honour, Messua, he is not unlike thy boy that was taken by the tiger.

Messua Let me look. (*Coming closer*) Indeed he is not. He is thinner, but he has the very look of my boy.

Priest What the Jungle has taken the Jungle has restored. Take the boy into thy house, Messua——

This is easier said than done, but Messua succeeds

—and forget not the priest who sees so far into the lives of men.

The crowd parts to let Mowgli and Messua through, then disperses

Buldeo Jungle filth!

The Lights fade to the interior of Messua's house

Messua You are so thin. You must be hungry. Hungry?

She mimes. Mowgli nods

Here.

She gives him some (imaginary) milk and some bread. Mowgli eats, drinks and demands more

More bread? (*She shows him*) "Bread."
Younger Mowgli Bed.
Messua No. "Bread."
Younger Mowgli Bread. (*He mimes drinking*)
Messua This—(*she gives him milk*)—"milk".
Younger Mowgli Milk. Bread, milk.

Mowgli eats again, closely observed by Messua. Mowgli shows interest in Messua's shoe

Messua Nathoo. O Nathoo. Dost thou not remember the day when I gave thee thy new shoes? (*She touches his foot*) No. Those feet have never worn shoes. But thou art very like my Nathoo, and thou shalt be my son.

Mowgli finishes eating. He asks about shoes. Messua supplies the word. Mowgli repeats his vocabulary. He finds the bed and asks about it. He repeats the word, questioning. Messua mimes the use of a bed and suggests that he sleep there. Mowgli will not sleep under a roof and runs outside. The Lights fade to exterior evening. Mowgli chooses a spot, pats the ground

Younger Mowgli Mowgli—bed.

He sees a fire burning outside the house. He moves towards it. Messua starts

Messua No! Fire!!
Younger Mowgli (*withdrawing his hand*) Fire.

Messua fetches a fire-pot, and shovel

Messua Fire-pot.
Younger Mowgli Fire-pot.

Messua shovels up some of the fire. She moves towards the house turns in the doorway

Messua Good-night—Mowgli.

Messua exits

Grey Brother enters. He sniffs, sneezes

Younger Mowgli Grey Brother!
Grey Brother This is a poor reward for following thee twenty miles. Thou smellest of woodsmoke and cattle—altogether like a man already.
Younger Mowgli Grey Brother, what news? What happened at the Council? Does Akela still live? What of Shere Khan?
Grey Brother Hold! Hold, Little Brother. Thou art like the Monkey-People who chatter and wait for no reply! Akela missed his kill.
Younger Mowgli And did the Pack kill him?
Grey Brother They would have, but none dared be the first to try. Shere Khan howled to find thee gone and when none could, or would, say where thou wert he and Tabaqui set off to find thee. They think thou art elsewhere in the Jungle and it will be some time before their thoughts bend

this way. But when they do, beware, little Frog-Brother, for Shere Khan has sworn he will lay thy bones in the Waingunga River.

Younger Mowgli There are two words to that. I also have made a little promise. But news is always good. I am tired tonight—very tired with new things, Grey Brother, but bring me the news always.

Grey Brother Thou wilt not forget that thou art a wolf? Men will not make thee forget?

Younger Mowgli Never. I will always remember those that I love, but also I will remember that I have been cast out of the Pack.

Grey Brother And that thou mayst be cast out of another pack. Men are only men, Little Brother, and their talk is like the talk of frogs on a pond. When I come down here again, I will wait for thee in the bamboos at the edge of the grazing ground.

Grey Brother exits

Younger Mowgli Fire!

Tableau. Sitar chord

SCENE 6

The Village

As the boy Younger Mowgli must now give way to the man, he takes on the job of narration, introducing the man Older Mowgli (who has played the part in the "Englishman" scenes), dressed in a dhoti

Younger Mowgli (*as Narrator*) For three months after that night Mowgli hardly ever left the village gate he was so busy learning the ways and customs of men. He had to wear a cloth about him which annoyed him horribly, and to learn about money, which he did not in the least understand, and about all the other matters which are so important to men but which the animals can somehow do without.

Younger Mowgli exits, leaving Older Mowgli

Narrator But he learnt and grew as strong in the ways of men as he was in the ways of the Jungle./Yet—as the man-cub had found his enemies in the Jungle so now the young man found his enemies in the village./One night he went to the great fig-tree——

The Lights fade to exterior evening light

—under which the men of the village would sit of an evening./

Head Man, Buldeo and Barber enter and sit

Head Man It was the village club and the Head Man/
Barber And the Barber (who knew all the gossip of the village)/
Buldeo And Old Buldeo, the village hunter, who owned a Tower musket/
Head Man Met and talked, and smoked their big hookahs until far into the night./

A Child brings on the hookahs

They told wonderful tales of gods and men and ghosts;/ and old Buldeo
told even more wonderful tales of the ways of beasts in the Jungle,/till the
eyes of the children sitting outside the circle bulged out of their heads./
Mowgli, who naturally knew something of what they were talking, had to
cover his face not to show that he was laughing,/while Buldeo, the Tower
musket across his knees, climbed from one wonderful story to another,/
and Mowgli's shoulders shook./Buldeo was explaining how the tiger that
had carried off Messua's son was a ghost tiger, and his body was
inhabited by the ghost of a wicked old money-lender, who had died some
years ago./

Buldeo And I know that this is true because Purun Dass always limped
from a blow that he got in a riot when his account-books were burned,
and the tiger that I speak of, he limps too, for the tracks of his pads are
unequal.

Head Man True.

Barber True. It must be true.

Older Mowgli Are all these tales such cobwebs and moon-talk? That tiger
limps because he was born lame, as everyone knows. To talk of the soul of
a money-lender in a beast that never had the courage of a jackal is child's
talk.

Buldeo Oho! It is the jungle-brat, is it? If thou art so wise better take his hide
to Khaniwara, for the Government has set a hundred rupees on his life.
Better still, do not talk when thy elders speak.

Older Mowgli (*rising and moving off*) All the evening I have lain here
listening and, except once or twice, Buldeo has not said a word of truth
concerning the jungle, which is at his very door. How then shall I believe
his tales of ghosts, gods and goblins which he says he has seen.

Head Man It is full time that boy went to herding.

Tableau. Sitar chord

SCENE 7

The Plain

*The Villagers remain onstage to narrate, adding subtle sound effects to
increase the atmosphere. Sitar music*

Narrator Herding in India is one of the laziest things in the world./ The
cattle move/and crunch,/and lie down,/and move on again./The sun
makes the rocks dance in the heat,/and a single kite whistles, almost out
of sight, overhead,/And the herd children sleep and wake and sleep again/
or sing long, long songs with quavers at the end of them,/and the day
seems longer than most people's whole lives./Then evening comes and the
children call,/and the cattle string across the grey plain back towards the
twinkling village lights./

The Villagers drift away over the preceding sentence, leaving only two. The music fades

Day after day Mowgli went through the village street in the dawn, riding on the back of Rama, the great herd-bull, and day after day he would drive them to the edge of the plain where the Waingunga River came out of the Jungle to seek news from Grey Brother./The village children were used to his strange ways and did not follow; nor did they ask why he carried a fire-pot with him, even on the hottest day, always having fire close by.

Wolf howl

Older Mowgli Grey Brother!

Grey Brother enters

Grey Brother, what news?

Grey Brother He has come back to this country and knows you are here. He crossed the ranges last night with Tabaqui, hot-foot on thy trail!

Older Mowgli I am not afraid of Shere Khan, but Tabaqui is very cunning.

Grey Brother Have no fear. I met Tabaqui in the dawn. Now he is telling all his wisdom to the kites, but he told me everything, before I broke his back. Shere Khan's plan is to wait for thee at the village gate, for thee and no-one else. He is lying up now, in the big, dry ravine of the Waingunga.

Older Mowgli Has he eaten today or does he hunt empty?

Grey Brother He killed, at dawn—a pig—and he has drunk too.

Older Mowgli Oh! Fool! Fool! What a cub's cub it is! Eaten, and drunk too, and he thinks that I shall wait untii he has slept! (*He thinks*) The big, dry ravine of the Waingunga ... (*He draws a plan in dust with his knife*) That opens up on to the plain not half a mile from here. I could take the herd round to the head of the ravine, but he would slink out at the foot. Grey Brother, canst thou cut the herd in two for me?

Grey Brother Not I alone, perhaps—but I have brought a wise helper.

Akela appears

Older Mowgli Akela! I knew thou wouldst not forget me! Come, we have big work in hand. Cut the herd in two—the cows and the calves together and the bulls and bullocks in the other half. Drive the bulls away to the left, Akela. Grey Brother drive the cows to the foot of the ravine. When the two halves of the herd smell tiger they will go mad with rage and ...

Akela And Shere Khan will be caught between them.

Grey Brother How far up the ravine shall we drive them?

Older Mowgli Till the sides are higher than Shere Khan can jump.

Akela But at the bend in the ravine one side drops. He will escape there!

Older Mowgli No, Akela. There he will meet his fate, for there I shall be with the friend of man I carry here in this pot. Away my brothers! It will be long before the Jungle forgets this day!

Akela Good hunting, Little Brother!

Grey Brother Good hunting!

Older Mowgli Good hunting both!

All three exit

SCENE 8

The Ravine

Slow, processional drumbeat

Four actors enter and kneel facing the audience. From the back of the auditorium four more actors file in carrying aloft life-size buffalo-heads. They take up positions behind the kneeling actors and freeze

Shere Khan enters, sleepily. He lies down and dozes. A bird is startled, Shere Khan raises his head but does not get up. Distant sounds of cattle. Once again he raises his head. He sniffs the air and is puzzled by the smell of the wind but thinks nothing of it

Shere Khan The village cattle have strayed from their grazing ground. But I have already eaten, and I shall eat again before the moon rises.

Older Mowgli calls, off. The chorus create an echo effect

Older Mowgli (*off*) Shere Khan! Cattle thief! Child-killer! Eater of frogs and rats! Shere Khan!
Shere Khan Who calls?
Older Mowgli (*off*) I, Mowgli! It is time to come to the Council Rock, Shere Khan. Down—hurry them down, Akela! Grey Brother move them up!

The cattle start to move in

Sniff the wind, Rama! On it you will smell the stench of tiger!

Rama bellows

Ha! Ha! Now thou knowest!

The following narration is taken by the eight members of cast who are kneeling and holding masks. As the kneeling actors finish their lines the masks are lowered over their heads. The narration is delivered with a growing urgency. The drumbeat quickens

Narrator The bulls took up Rama's cry/and the cows and calves answered it from the other end of the ravine/and the torrent of sharp horns, foaming muzzles and staring eyes/whirled down the ravine like boulders in flood-time;/the weaker beasts being shouldered to the sides of the ravine where they tore up the creepers./They knew what business was before them/—the terrible charge of the stampeding herd,/against which no tiger can hope to stand.

Older Mowgli enters above, carrying a fire-pot

Older Mowgli Now! Shere Khan! Now is thy moment come! Dost thou know me?
Shere Khan Man-cub!

Older Mowgli Ay, the man-cub that was to be thy prey! And like a true-born man I have with me the red flower, see!

Shere Khan tries to climb up to Mowgli. Mowgli draws a "branch" from the fire-pot and thrusts it in Shere Khan's face. Shere Khan howls

Roar well, cattle-killer! It is thy last chance! Choose thy death, Shere Khan, the cattle whose calves thou hast killed or the naked babe thou snatched from his mother!

Again Shere Khan attacks. Again he is driven back. The cattle close in, moving to the beat. Finally he screams again "Man-cub" and makes a huge effort to get at Mowgli. He catches Mowgli off-guard and knocks him to the ground. Mowgli escapes his pounce but has lost his fire-brand. He climbs back up to where he has left his fire-pot, hotly pursued by Shere Khan. Mowgli grabs another branch and hits Shere Khan once, twice, a third time. Shere Khan pitches forward in slow motion, is tossed in the air and finally falls. A moment's silence, then . . .

Quick Akela! Break them up. Scatter them or they will be fighting one another. Drive them away Akela. Hai, Rama! Hai, hai! Hai! My children. Softly now, softly! It is all over.

The Ravine clears

Mowgli jumps down

Akela and Grey Brother retire upstage and lie down

Brothers, that was a dog's death. But he would never have shown fight. His hide will look well on the Council Rock. We must get to work swiftly.

Mowgli starts to skin Shere Khan with the help of the Wolves. After the initial effort he sends the Wolves away

Akela and Grey Brother retire upstage and lie down

Buldeo enters

Buldeo What is this folly? To think that thou canst skin a tiger! Did the cattle kill him? It is the lame tiger, too, and there is a hundred rupees on his head. Well, well, we will overlook your letting the herd run off, and perhaps I will give thee one of the rupees of the reward when I take the skin to Khaniwara. (*He takes out flint and steel to singe the tiger's whiskers*)

Older Mowgli Hum! So thou wilt take the hide to Khaniwara for the reward? Now it is in my mind that I need the skin for my own use. Heh! Old man, take away that fire!

Buldeo What talk is this to the chief hunter of the village? Thy luck and the stupidity of thy cattle have helped thee to this kill. The tiger has just fed or he would have gone twenty miles by this time. Thou canst not even skin him properly, Little Beggar-brat, and forsooth I, Buldeo, must be told not to singe his whiskers. Mowgli, I will not give thee one anna of the reward, but only a very big beating. Leave the carcass!

Older Mowgli By the Bull that bought me must I stay babbling to an old ape all noon. Here, Akela, this man plagues me.

Akela and Grey Brother spring from cover, pinning Buldeo to the ground

Yes, thou art altogether right, Buldeo. Thou wilt not give me one anna of the reward. There is an old war between this tiger and myself—a very old war. And I have won.

Buldeo Maharaj? Great King?

Older Mowgli Yes?

Buldeo I am but a man. I did not know that thou wast anything more than a herd-boy. May I rise up and go away, or will thy servants tear me to pieces?

Older Mowgli Go, and peace go with thee. Only another time do not meddle with my game. Let him go Akela, Grey Brother.

Buldeo edges away. He tries to pick up his musket, is chased off by Wolves

Ye spoke truth, Grey Brother. Some men may be wise and good but others are as foolish as the deer that run into the tiger's jaws. Come, one last pull and we are done.

The Chorus enters upstage

Mowgli, Akela and Grey Brother strip the skin from the tiger's carcass, roll the body off it, and Mowgli folds it into a bundle

Older Mowgli Brothers, let us take this to the Council Rock to show that my word is my word. Then it may be that the story of Mowgli and his brothers will go on—but certainly the story of Shere Khan is finished.

Older Mowgli exits

Faces in the dark. A single light on Shere Khan

Face 1 What of the hunting, hunter bold?

Abdul enters by statue of Demon. He finds Amira's veil draped over its face

Shere Khan Brother, the watch was long and cold.

Face 2 What of the quarry ye went to kill?

Mowgli and Amira enter by statue of Krishna. They wave to Abdul

Shere Khan Brother he walks in the Jungle still.

Face 3 Where is the power that made your pride?

Mowgli and Amira kiss. Abdul hides his face in the veil

Shere Khan Brother, it bleeds from my flank and side.

The Lights fade on Mowgli, Amira and Abdul. The Faces all snap on their lights

Face 4 Why do ye sleep, yet draw no breath?

The Face lights snap off, leaving only Shere Khan lit

Shere Khan Brother, my sleep is the sleep of death.

Tableau. Sitar chord. Black-out

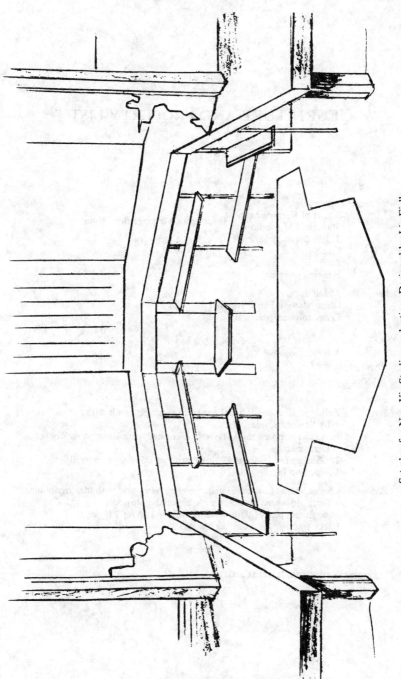

Set plan for New Vic Studio production. Designed by Liz Fjelle

FURNITURE AND PROPERTY LIST

ACT I

SCENE 1

On stage: Upper level:
Statue of Krishna far L ⎫
Statue of Demon far R ⎭ These remain onstage throughout
Table. *On it:* plate, knife, fork, bottle, glass, rifle
Chair
Lower level:
Hanging creepers

Personal: **Abdul**: dagger
Older Mowgli: hunting-knife
Faces: torches (practical)

SCENES 2, 3 and 4

No props required

SCENE 5

Set: Full-head tiger mask (idealized face, no stripes) with latex "stone" cover
by Krishna statue
Full-head elephant mask, lavishly decorated, with latex "stone" cover on
Demon statue
2 rolled-up fabric "rivers"—long strips of shiny blue material
1 folded-up fabric "pool"

Personal: **Chorus**: masks (2-dimensional, wooden, hand-held with idealized animal
faces), idealized branches with leaves and blossoms
Men: flutes/spears (plain, black dowel-rods about 2'6" long)
Bucks 1 and **2**: full-head buck masks

SCENE 6

Off stage: Nuts, twigs, leaves **(Cast)**

SCENE 7

Set: As Scene 1 plus a rifle

ACT II

SCENE 1

Set: As Act I, Scene 7

Off stage: Rifle (**Abdul**)

Personal: **Abdul**: dagger

SCENE 2

Personal: **Older Mowgli**: flute, hunting-knife

SCENES 3 and 4

No props required

SCENE 5

Personal: **Faces**: torches (practical)

For Village (*page 33*), *set:*
             Bowl, jug, plate inside **Messua**'s "hut"
             Fire-pot, shovel outside

Personal: **Man**: hoe, food in basket
             Buldeo: musket

SCENE 6

Off stage: 3 hookahs (**Child**)

Personal: **Buldeo**: musket
             Older Mowgli: hunting-knife

SCENE 7

Personal: **Older Mowgli**: hunting-knife, fire-pot

SCENE 8

Set: **Amira**'s orange veil over statue of Demon

Personal: **Older Mowgli**: Hunting-knife, fire-pot
             4 actors: buffalo heads
             Faces: torches (practical)
             Buldeo: musket, flint, steel

The major props (statues, masks etc) for this play may be hired from:
   Bristol Old Vic Wardrobe and Furniture Hire Dept.,
   Colston Hall Vaults
   Colston Street
   Bristol 1

LIGHTING PLOT

Practical fittings required: small torches for **Faces**

A bungalow verandah, the Jungle

ACT I, SCENE 1

To open: Moody evening light on verandah

| Cue 1 | **Older Mowgli:** "Where to begin?" | (Page 3) |
| | *Slow fade to sunset* | |

| Cue 2 | **Older Mowgli:** "Then I shall tell thee." | (Page 4) |
| | *Fade to black-out* | |

| Cue 3 | **Faces:** "That keep the Jungle Law!" | (Page 4) |
| | *Bring up light on* **Narrator** | |

ACT I, SCENE 2

To open: Light on **Narrator**, evening light on lower level

| Cue 4 | **Father Wolf:** "But what will the Pack say?" | (Page 7) |
| | *Snap up bright lighting* | |

ACT I, SCENE 3

To open: As Cue 4

| Cue 5 | **Narrator:** "... to the Council Rock." | (Page 7) |
| | *Fade to moonlight* | |

ACT I, SCENE 4

To open: Bring up bright daylight

| Cue 6 | **Narrator:** "... into the heart of the Jungle." | (Page 11) |
| | *Increase to brighter level* | |

ACT I, SCENE 5

To open: As Cue 6

| Cue 7 | **Hathi:** "... and I will tell it." | (Page 13) |
| | *Fade to spot on* **Younger Mowgli** *and* **Hathi** *(upper level)* | |

| Cue 8 | **Hathi:** "... the First of the Elephants ..." | (Page 13) |
| | *Bring up lights on statues and lower level* | |

| Cue 9 | **Hathi:** "... to meet the hairless one." | (Page 16) |
| | *Fade out* **Hathi**'s *spot* | |

Cue 10 **Men** thrust at **Tiger**. Thunder   (Page 16)
    Black-out; pause, then lights up on **Hathi** *and* **Younger Mowgli**

Cue 11 **Younger Mowgli**: "... being of the Free People."   (Page 16)
    Bring up lights on lower level—bright daylight

ACT I, SCENE 6

To open: As Cue 11

Cue 12 **Bagheera**: "... to the Cold Lairs."   (Page 23)
    Fade to black-out

ACT I, SCENE 7

To open: evening light on verandah

Cue 13 **Older Mowgli**: "I shall serve Queen Victoria."   (Page 23)
    Fade to black-out

ACT II, SCENE 1

To open: Night—moonlight on verandah

Cue 14 **Abdul** exits, followed by **Gisborne**   (Page 24)
    Black-out

ACT II, SCENE 2

To open: Black-out

Cue 15 When ready   (Page 24)
    Bring up moonlight on lower level

Cue 16 **Older Mowgli**: "... to the Cold Lairs."   (Page 25)
    Fade to black-out

ACT II, SCENE 3

To open: Spot on **Narrator**

Cue 17 As other **Narrators** speak   (Page 25)
    Widen lighting to take them in

Cue 18 **Narrator**: "... particularly pleased with themselves." (Page 26)
    Bring up general lighting—daylight

Cue 19 **Baloo**: "... and we will go home."   (Page 29)
    Fade to black-out

ACT II, SCENE 4

To open: Spot on **Narrator**

Cue 20 **Narrator**: "... he said to Mowgli——"   (Page 29)
    Bring up warm daylight

Cue 21 **Bagheera**: "... frog-hunt of thine ten years ago." (Page 32)
    Fade to black-out

ACT II, Scene 5

To open: Snap up spot on **Narrator**

Cue 22   **Narrator**: "... heart was hot within him."   (Page 32)
          Bring up dim, green lighting on **Younger Mowgli**

Cue 23   As verse starts and during it   (Page 32)
          Alternate coloured lighting, centred on **Mowgli**, *changing colours*
          with the beat of the verse and drum

Cue 24   At end of verse   (Page 33)
          Return to central green lighting

Cue 25   **Younger Mowgli** moves as if to part the branches at the forest
          edge   (Page 33)
          Bring up bright, bare daylight

Cue 26   **Buldeo**: "Jungle filth!"   (Page 33)
          Fade to interior of **Messua**'s "hut"

Cue 27   **Younger Mowgli** runs outside "hut"   (Page 34)
          Fade to exterior evening light

ACT II, Scene 6

To open: Bright lights for narration

Cue 28   **Narrator**: "... he went to the great fig-tree——"   (Page 35)
          Fade to exterior evening light

ACT II, Scene 7

To open: Bright daylight

No cues

ACT II, Scene 8

To open: Daylight

Cue 29   As drum beats   (Page 38)
          Dim lights slightly with drum beat

Cue 30   **Shere Khan** pitches forward   (Page 39)
          Fade to spot c

Cue 31   **Older Mowgli**: "Quick Akela! Break them up."   (Page 39)
          Return to previous lighting

Cue 32   **Older Mowgli** exits   (Page 40)
          Fade to spot on **Shere Khan**

Cue 33   **Face 1**: "What of the hunting, hunter bold?"   (Page 40)
          Bring up lights on statues

Cue 34   **Shere Khan**: "... from my flank and side."   (Page 40)
          Fade lights on statues

Cue 35   **Shere Khan**: "... the sleep of death."   (Page 40)
          Black-out

EFFECTS PLOT

Many of the effects listed below may be performed live on stage, as are all the animal noises listed in the text—see Production Notes

ACT I

Cue 1	Black-out	(Page 4)
	Low drumbeat	
Cue 2	**Father Wolf**: ". . . will the Pack say?" (*Tableau*)	(Page 7)
	Sitar chord	
Cue 3	**Akela**: ". . . one of the Free People."	(Page 9)
	Sitar chord	
Cue 4	**Tha**: "Seek and ye shall find."	(Page 15)
	Pipe plays, off	
Cue 5	**Tiger** kills **Man**	(Page 16)
	Thunder	
Cue 6	**Men** thrust spears at **Tiger**	(Page 16)
	Thunder	
Cue 7	**Younger Mowgli**: ". . . being of the Free People."	(Page 16)
	Thunder, rain	
Cue 8	**Younger Mowgli** plays "invisible" pipe	(Page 17)
	Pipe music	
Cue 9	**Younger Mowgli** blows pipe in **Baloo**'s ear	(Page 18)
	Loud blast of pipe music	
Cue 10	**Bagheera**: ". . . to the Cold Lairs."	(Page 23)
	Sitar chord, then fast sitar music to cover scene change	
Cue 11	When ready for Scene 7	(Page 23)
	Cut sitar music	

ACT II

Cue 12	As Scene 2 opens	(Page 24)
	Flute music—continue for a few seconds	
Cue 13	**Older Mowgli**: ". . . to the Cold Lairs."	(Page 25)
	Sitar chord	
Cue 14	**Baloo**: ". . . and we will go home."	(Page 29)
	Sitar chord	
Cue 15	**Bagheera**: ". . . of thine ten years ago."	(Page 32)
	Sitar chord	

MADE AND PRINTED IN GREAT BRITAIN BY
LATIMER TREND & COMPANY LTD, PLYMOUTH
MADE IN ENGLAND